Meatlo

Mastering Emotional Intelligence

Riley Inge Jr.

Copyright © 2023 by **Riley Inge Jr.**

All rights reserved. No part of this publication may be reproduced, distributed or transmitted in any form or by any means, without prior written permission.

Riley Inge Jr.

Publisher's Note: This is a work of fiction. Names, characters, places, and incidents are a product of the author's imagination. Locales and public names are sometimes used for atmospheric purposes. Any resemblance to actual people, living or dead, or to businesses, companies, events, institutions, or locales is completely coincidental.

Book Layout © 2017 BookDesignTemplates.com

Emotional Intelligence/ Riley Inge Jr. -- 1st ed.
ISBN 9798876171771

My Village:
Tyrnita Moore-Inge, Riley J. Inge, Tiger O. Woods-Inge, Peyton Engel, Geneva Robinson, Riley Inge Sr., Betty Kirby, Alisha Clifton, Onyx Inge, Brittany Inge, Josh Inge, Larry Robinson, Darran Clifton Sr., Kelly Inge, Wallace Kirby, and Juell Dorton.
Thank you all for your love, support, and constant inspiration.
I love you all.

The most important thing is to try and inspire people so that they can be great in whatever they want to do. Everything negative- pressures, challenges- is all an opportunity for me to rise.

—KOBE BRYANT

Contents

Emotional Intelligence 5
Changing your Circle 7
Never let loyalty make a fool of you 9
The Beauty of Silence 11
Self-Visualization 13
Speak Truth 15
The silence of our friends is unforgettable 17
How to date an entreprenuer 19
Raised vibrations elimanates life's non-essentials 21
The cost of not following your heart 25
Never stop doing your best 27
Stronger than Yesterday 29
Remaining Calm 31
You don't get to decide how soon others heal 33
Tough times and living right 39
Never too old to start a new dream 45
Peter vs. Judas 49
Prepared for the unpredictable 51
Obscurity is Acceptable 57
Strong Crews 61
Betrayal is a part of the plan 65
The theory of right and wrong is Timeless 67
Every choice comes with an invoice 69
Final Thoughts 77

Emotional Intelligence

Emotional Intelligence

Jay Z said, "If I shoot you, I'm brainless, but if you shoot me, you're famous."

In some situations, it can be beneficial to choose not to react or respond immediately. Instead, it may be wiser to maintain composure, take a step back, and assess the situation before responding. This approach allows for a more thoughtful and measured response, potentially avoiding unnecessary conflict or escalating the situation further.

It highlights the value of restraint and choosing when and how to respond to achieve a more favorable outcome.

There are people that want to know what it will take for you to lose control. It does not matter, man or woman, they will test you. Beware of these toxic people that enjoy confrontation and arguments over peace and harmony. They think by saying or doing something that might get you out of character, it will show them what you're made of. The problem is you can never take back an action that you display so be very careful what you show others. A good quote is, "Bad Boys move in silence". Remember, just because you haven't done anything doesn't mean you won't do anything. Because the most dangerous person is the one NOT talking. Just know when you SHINE, because Allah's love for you is radiant, everyone will watch you. I learned at a very young age that there are people everywhere paying attention to what I'm doing. Either to use me as a positive example or

awaiting my downfall to proclaim they knew I wasn't as good as I projected myself to be. I've heard stories that involved my name told by people that I once loved or truly respected. Yes, it hurts but it's important to weigh all the options. And weighing your options can be achieved by calming your heart rate and applying logic to the situation. Ask yourself these questions, "what am I jeopardizing by reacting to this"? Will it be worth it? What will I lose by not responding? Everything isn't worth your time, effort, or energy. The devil is working to distract you.
STAY SOLID ALWAYS.

Changing your Circle
Emotional Intelligence

How do you have 20 friends to go drinking with and not 1 to do business with?
It's very important to surround yourself with like-minded individuals who share similar goals and aspirations. I've learned that having many friends for social activities may not necessarily translate into having professional connections or business opportunities. To rectify this, you must evaluate and potentially change your social circle to include individuals who are interested in and engaged in business or entrepreneurial endeavors. By doing so, you may increase your chances of finding people to collaborate with or pursue business ventures together. Your friends should be a part of your development. Use your friends for more than laughs and a good time. Our friends should motivate us to do things that take our lives to the next level. Our "friends" should be our support system, otherwise what exactly makes them your friend? What makes you want to spend time with people that take things from you (like your time) with a smile. Try talking to your friends to see what they inspire to be, inquire about what they're doing to attain their goal. Can you be helpful? One of the greatest titles I ever held was "teammate ". I would literally do ANYTHING to assure my teammates success because I always liked being around successful people. My Coach once told me that winning a championship is better than the best sex you'll ever have

because the feeling lasts longer. There's no greater feeling than WINNING with people you care for.

Look at your friends and ask yourself are WE WINNING or are we LOSING?

Note: You are losing if you are not progressing, and it may be time to change your circle!

Never let your loyalty make a fool of you

Emotional Intelligence

Never should you blindly and unquestionably remain loyal in a way that leads to being taken advantage of or being deceived.

Loyalty should be balanced with critical thinking and discernment to avoid being exploited or deceived by those who may not have your best interests at heart. In essence, it encourages individuals to maintain a cautious and thoughtful approach to loyalty.

Don't get me wrong, being loyal is the right thing to do, just remember everyone doesn't deserve your allegiance. An old friend once said to me, Riley your problem is you expect others to treat you the way you treat them, and you get let down whenever they come up short. I've really struggled with this in my life. At first, I thought he was right! I do get let down often because I expect people to do for me like I would do for them. Because to the best of my ability, I try to do right for all people I encounter. Giving each person the best of me. I've had others tell me, how can you show so much love for people that don't show up for you the way you show up or celebrate them. I find that kind of energy distracting. I've never done anything for anyone expecting something back in return.

But there are times that I consider the following:
Would someone continue to invest money into a stock that doesn't pay off? I mean everyone knows playing the stock market is a gamble and people do lose their money. But the question is, would you continue to put more money into a stock that doesn't pay off for you? Similarly, it's like being loyal to people or a situation that's not productive for you. So, I now conclude that my friend was wrong because I deserve to be treated by others the way I treat them. But more importantly, it's up to me to decide who deserves my loyalty.

The Beauty of Silence
Emotional Intelligence

One of the things I enjoy doing the most is surprising people. I've been called "sneaky" and "secretive", but in truth I love catching people's natural reaction to something they never saw coming. I've done this all my life. Friends and associates were bewildered to find me in the classroom working as a teacher when I struggled the way I did in school. It's even more amazing to see how I'm able to connect with youth or even more so "troubled youth".

In short, I delight in doing the unexpected. Likewise, remaining calm when others expect a volatile response is unforeseen.

It can be empowering and admirable to remain calm and composed in situations where others expect you to be angry or upset. It suggests that maintaining inner peace and not succumbing to external pressures can be a beautiful and powerful response. Silence highlights the strength and grace found in controlling one's emotions and choosing not to engage in expected negativity. Additionally, remaining calm avoids doing something you'll later regret. Especially during a time when you're solid and you do right by people, but you get hurt because of individuals challenged by self-hate. These are people who struggle with personal demons and can't understand how it is you're always winning, or that you're loved. And when these same people tell a lie against you that causes other people to believe that untruth, the natural inclination would be to clear your name and expose the one telling the falsehood against you.

However, what if you remained silent?

Now, I get it. There are some things you'll need to rectify! But remember everyone doesn't deserve your energy. Plus, it's a good practice to "keep receipts!" Meaning it's good to remember who said what, who was vocal, and who was quiet. This should make it easier for you to remain silent when you want to scream your innocence.

As you go forward, remember this phrase: SUBHAN ALLAH.

Allah is perfect or Glory be to God.

His Glory is the beauty that can be revealed in our silence.

Self-Visualization

Emotional Intelligence

Self-visualization encourages individuals to imagine themselves as they aspire to be, and then take action to transform their vision into reality. It emphasizes the importance of self-reflection, goal setting, and actively working towards personal growth and development.
Allah has given you the tools to create whatever it is you want to create. But before you create it, you need to be able to see it. There are things I cannot visualize because it's not for me to manifest it, but if you can see It......you have what it takes to get it done. So, take some time and think about the person you want to be and not the things you want to have. If you can become the person you want to be, that person can attract the things you want for yourself. If the person you want to be can attract all the things you want, then you must work on becoming "THAT PERSON". Before you can work on becoming that person you will need to take the time to reflect on who you are today! If you find that a large gap exists between your present state and who you desire to be- you will need to set some goals to measure your progress. Your goals should be small (because it's the little steps that get you over the mountain), measurable, and attainable.

13

For example, if someone aspires to play in the NBA..... did they dribble their ball today? Improve on the use of their left hand? These are the examples of enacting small goals needed to achieve the dream of personal development. Become the you that you visualize obtaining all that is associated with being that person.

Speak Truth
Emotional Intelligence

The only people that will be mad at you for speaking the truth are those that want to live in the lie. Alternatively, they become upset or angry with you for telling the truth while preferring to live in a falsehood or denial than to confront what's real. Speaking the truth can be a courageous and necessary act, even if it is met with resistance or backlash. It emphasizes the importance of honesty and integrity, even when it challenges the beliefs or comfort of others. Social media today is very dangerous! Most of the lives showcased on this platform are artificial.

This reminds me of one of Jay Z's best albums.

American Gangster and his song: Ignorant Shit

"They're all actors.
   Looking at themselves in the mirror backwards
Can't even face themselves, don't fear no rappers
   They're all weirdos, DeNiro's in Practice
So, don't believe everything your earlobe captures
   It's mostly backwards
Unless it happens to be as accurate as me
   And everything said in song you happen to see
Then actually, believe half of what you see
   None of what you hear even if it's spat by me."

Instead of living artificially as Jay-Z describes, live a life that may not be ideal, but is the reality of who you are.

The silence of our friends is unforgettable

Emotional Intelligence

When reflecting on our lives, we are more likely to remember the lack of support or inaction from our friends during challenging times, rather than the negative words or actions of our enemies. It underscores the significance of friendship and the impact that the absence of support can have on us. It implies that the silence or indifference of our friends can be hurtful and leave a lasting impression. The statement serves as a reminder to value and appreciate the presence and support of true friends in our lives.

I talked earlier about keeping receipts. Alternatively, the words and actions of people around you are proof of conduct. However, the words of your enemies won't matter much to you because usually we know where the energy comes from. But the silence or lack of support from those that you love will hit you like a ton of bricks.

I had a friend who I really loved like a family member. In fact, our families were blended. I treated his family like my own and his family handled me the same. The demise of that relationship materialized when he withheld his support instead of vouching for me. It only required him to speak about the things he knew about me. Knowing that I'm trustworthy, honest, of high character and integrity. But he said nothing, and it affected our connection. Man! He was close enough to the situation to make that relationship work.

What became apparent was although I saw him as family, and I felt protective of him and all that he loved; he had boundaries with me. The relationship was fine if we were at the bar drinking our lives away, but he didn't treat me like the blood relative I felt he was to me. Sound familiar? I just spoke about loyalty, and he no longer deserved mine. Yet, I decided to remain calm and quiet and love him from a distance.

In the end you'll need to learn how to protect yourself and your feelings from those we claim to be our friends.

How to date and entrepreneur

Emotional Intelligence

Dating an entrepreneur can be challenging due to their demanding lifestyle and dedication to their work. One option is to become an assistant to the entrepreneur. Actively contributing to their goals and supporting their endeavors. On the other hand, if someone is not willing or able to fulfill that role, it implies they should step aside and allow the entrepreneur to focus on their work without distractions. In other words, become an assistant or get out the way! Ultimately, it is important to understand and accommodate the unique lifestyle and priorities of an entrepreneur in a romantic relationship. You have no idea how scary and difficult it is to go into business ALONE! I spoke earlier about having friends around you that support your vision and want to see you win by CONTRIBUTING. One person who encapsulates this and who happens to be one of my favorite basketball players is Draymond Green of the Golden State Warriors. What I love about his game is that he contributes to winning in a MAJOR WAY, yet the common fan can't appreciate his role on that team. They also don't like his brashness but that's another story. You cannot build a house without nails. Yes, the hammer, wood, saw, metal, and other things are important but where would that house be without nails? Draymond contributes to winning the way nails contribute to holding things together. But the beauty in it is that when you see the house the nails become minutia.

You can contribute to helping an entrepreneur in a Draymond Green kind of way. The unobtrusive supporter.

Raised vibrations eliminate life's non-essentials

Emotional Intelligence

When you elevate your energy or "vibration" by focusing on positivity, personal growth, and pursuing what aligns with your authentic self, things or people that are not in alignment with your newfound state will naturally fade away or leave your life. As you raise your own energetic frequency, you may outgrow certain situations, relationships, or circumstances that no longer serve your higher purpose or resonate with your newfound mindset. The importance of personal growth and self-discovery is in attracting relationships and manifesting experiences that are in alignment with your true self.

We were all designed with a purpose in mind by the creator. (S.A.W.) **Subhanahu wa ta'ala-** This Arabic phrase translates into "**May He be praised and exalted**" or more simply put that all praises are for him alone. Which means that each of us was designed to do something remarkable, even life changing, and Allah is arrogant. I say this because he put these great attributes in us all to make himself look like the ALMIGHTY!! ONLY HE could create the heavens, the earth, the animals, the seas, our parents, you, and me! Some of us can tap into what we were designed to do that ultimately gives our Creator recognition. Others are surrounded by so many distractions that they end up chasing their own tails like a confused dog missing the opportunity to do so. As mentioned before, there's so many distractions with social media, relationships, tv, etc…...that you can lose your focus. This is why you must spend time with YOURSELF, meditate and ask Allah what it is that you're meant to do with your life. Ask for clarity! Life is hard, but it's much easier when you know where you're going. For instance, imagine driving to another town you've never been to without any directions. Or consider the fact that each birthday you have is a new experience for you. As I write this book today, I'm 49 years old, I've never been 50 in my life. I have no idea what it's like to be 50 or 60 years old. What I am saying is Allah has the knowledge we need to succeed. Get into Him.

There's a saying that goes "youth is wasted on the young". Alternatively, the statement declares that young people often don't fully appreciate or take advantage of the opportunities, energy, and vitality that come with being youthful. It implies that with age and experience, individuals may develop a greater understanding and appreciation for their youth, realizing the missed potential or opportunities they had in their younger years. It serves as a reminder to make the most of one's youth and not take it for granted, as it is a time of vibrancy and possibility. When a person learns to communicate with God at a young age their older years will be so much easier for them. Jay Z said in his song (Family Feud- 4:44) "I told my wife the spiritual shit really works Alhamdulillah." Alhamdulillah is an Arabic word, which is also called Tamid in the native Arabic language. It means "praise be to God," and at times it is interpreted as "thanks to God,". What makes this lyric remarkable is that it contrasts his musical statements made in his youth. In his older music he mocked religion and his understanding of it displaying youthful arrogance as if he could do all these great things on his own. With age, Jay-Z seems to have raised his vibrations. His understanding reflects the power of meditation and communicating with THE MOST HIGH. However, you who are reading may not be young, but to someone who is 80 or 90- someone 49 or 50 is considered youthful. In other words, starting from where you are in communicating with God will still afford you the opportunity to raise your personal vibrations no matter your age. There's always someone who has lived longer than you!

The cost of not following your heart
Emotional Intelligence

If you choose not to pursue what truly inspires or fulfills you, you may end up living with regret and longing for the rest of your life. Ignoring the desires of your heart and settling for a path that doesn't align with your passions or dreams can lead to a sense of unfulfillment and dissatisfaction. It's important to listen to your inner voice, take risks, and pursue what genuinely brings you joy and purpose, even if it involves stepping outside of your comfort zone.

Earlier I mentioned that you should communicate with God early and often. In addition, it is here where your dreams can become a reality. However, there are caveats. You must work on yourself and ask for clarity in what is your purpose. Finally, you must understand that on the other side of that purpose is GREATNESS because Allah already placed the tools within you to be exceptional!

Here's another caveat. While some may believe it to be true, your purpose is not to be rich! However, perhaps if you tap into what your purpose truly is, there may be riches for you on the other side. What's most important to consider is that God did not create us to be rich or poor.

Whatever may be your purpose it's important to consider that discovery starts with communicating with the Most High. And I'm speaking of more than communicating with God just before you go to bed or before you bite your sandwich. I'm saying talk to him frequently. It's the people that you associate with the most that know you the best. If you have constant communication with God, he will vouch for you when it's necessary and will match your energy! Allahu Akbar: Arabic for "Allah is most great," or "God is great." It is used as a call to prayer. Begin your conversation with that! Because not following your heart highlights the potential consequences of ignoring its desires and God's design for your life.

Never stop doing your best
Emotional Intelligence

The value of one's work or actions should not solely depend on external validation or acknowledgment. Instead, doing your best emphasizes the importance of personal integrity, self-motivation, and a commitment to giving your best effort in everything you do. The intrinsic satisfaction and personal growth that come from consistently doing your best are more significant than any external recognition or credit that may or may not be given.

I attempt to approach each situation by giving the best of myself. Being a former athlete, one of the things that made me a standout was my competitive spirit. I learned to compete against myself by practicing against myself every day. As I spent time alone trying to perfect my craft it also built within me the work ethic to try my best no matter who was around or who was watching. This is the very definition of integrity. Integrity is the quality of being honest, having strong moral principles, and adhering to ethical values. It involves consistently acting in a trustworthy and honorable manner, even when no one is watching. Individuals with integrity demonstrate consistency between their words and actions, and they prioritize doing what they believe is right, even in challenging situations. Integrity is highly valued as it establishes trust, credibility, and respect in personal and professional relationships. It is a fundamental aspect of ethical behavior and serves as a guiding principle for making decisions and conducting oneself with honesty and fairness. If you bring this kind of approach to all that you do, you are bound to find success.

Stronger than Yesterday
Emotional Intelligence

"Stronger than yesterday" is a phrase often used to express personal growth, progress, and resilience. Remember I talked about setting small attainable goals to reach your mark? Stronger than yesterday is very key to achieving that goal. It implies that one has overcome challenges learned from experiences and become stronger as a result.

The idea of continuous improvement becomes the mindset of striving to be better each day. It serves as a reminder to focus on personal development, building upon past experiences, and embracing the strength gained from overcoming obstacles. It encourages individuals to keep pushing forward, even in the face of adversity, with the belief that they can become stronger and more resilient with each passing day.

I had a teammate that I played with in Finland. He was slightly older than me and as silly as he was, I learned something from him. Our coach would require some ridiculous training exercises in the preseason to get us into the best shape possible. I can remember one day being confused and a bit distraught by what we were doing because it involved so much running. I heard my teammate say, "nothing lasts forever". My focus was on the laborious effort of running, so I was confused by his statement. But he kept talking and said, "I know we're running a lot but sooner or later he has to blow his whistle, and this has to end." That concept has stayed with me all my life. Whenever I'm dealing with a difficult moment, I tell myself nothing lasts forever. I assure myself that just like that day of constant running I will also conquer whatever feat or obstacle that is placed in front of me. Because at the end of the day, my one goal is to be stronger than yesterday. Let that be your goal as well.

Oh! As a personal note: LET YOUR KIDS PLAY SPORTS! There are so many life lessons that come from being a part of a team.

Remaining Calm
Emotional Intelligence

Learning how to remain calm is one of the valuable lessons in life. Maintaining composure, even in challenging or stressful situations, can lead to better outcomes and personal well-being. As a former basketball player, I was usually the best player on my team. I was cheered at home games and booed while playing as the visiting team in other places. I realized that I enjoyed playing on the road in front of strangers more than playing at home in front of my family and friends. Here's why. The booing crowds became a calming noise that allowed me to focus on the objective and my teammates more. By staying calm, one can think more clearly, make rational decisions, and effectively navigate through difficulties. It also highlights the importance of emotional intelligence, self-control, and the ability to manage one's emotions.

I'm a huge Will Smith and Chris Rock fan, so it literally broke my heart to see what happened at the Oscars back in 2021. I'm speaking in the literal sense right now because I can remember how there were so many people (mainly women) that supported Will Smith's actions. Weirdly, I don't know either brother personally, yet my mood was affected drastically. I was noticeably sad and bothered by what had transpired between the two superstars. I've followed Will Smith's whole career since 1985 or 87 and he always seemed personable, funny, intelligent, and poised. But on this day, he lost his gracefulness.

When you allow emotions to get the better of logic bad things can happen. I remember a time when I lost my poise. I secretly dated a woman that I cared about very much, and I learned that she slept with one of my friends who was unaware of our relationship status. I lost my self-possession and became outraged as I broke items throughout her house. If she had called the police on me, I surely would've gone to court and probably jail for destruction of property. Although I was very hurt by her actions, I still had no right to respond the way I did.

Cultivating a sense of inner calmness can contribute to personal growth, improved relationships, and overall resilience in the face of life's challenges.

You don't get to decide how soon others heal

Emotional Intelligence

If you have caused harm to someone, it is not your place to dictate or control how they heal from that harm. It is important to respect their autonomy and give them the space and support they need to heal in their own way. I tell myself this almost every day because I'm far from perfect and I know I've hurt others through my actions. I'm a reactionary person therefore when I do something hurtful usually, I'm reacting to my own hurt that was caused by the other person. In other words, I'm a tit for tat kind of guy which in some cases can be very petty. But if I dig a little deeper, I think this mentality goes back to guidelines often enforced while participating in team sports. I always tried to stay within the regulations and compete through the fairness of the established rules. So, in my life if I feel like personal situations become unfair, I look for ways to re-establish the balance of fairness. That's a fancy way of saying I can be petty. While this is how I am wired, I equally understand the saying that goes two wrongs don't make a right. Ultimately, matching energy can cause harm and forces us to allow others time to adjust to the hurt we've caused.
And I've learned to stop rushing things that needed time to grow. This valuable lesson creates time for things to grow and develop naturally which can lead to better outcomes and more fulfilling experiences. **Masha'Allah**, Ma shaa **Allah** is an

Arabic phrase that means "God has willed" or "as God willing". In my later years, especially since I converted to Islam in 2019, I'm learning to simply submit to the will of Allah because I'm so flawed and God is perfectly unflawed. I've learned how important it is to be patient and allow things to progress at their own pace, rather than trying to force or rush them. This is especially so with wounds I may have intentionally or unintentionally inflicted on others.

I've been estranged from my youngest child for 8 years. This was the result of a broken or distant relationship with his mother. Being estranged often involves a lack of communication or emotional connection between parties. I've gone back and forth to court trying to establish myself in my son's life and although I would receive the successful verdict, I was seeking I'd never get the desired outcome or cooperation from the other parent. Consequently, depression, sadness, loneliness, helplessness, pain, anxiety, were many of the emotions I endured. Going back to court became useless in my opinion because no one would enforce the verdict. As hurt as I was, I thought maybe I should remove myself from the situation and allow her to heal from what she felt and hope that her heart would become open to allow me a spot in my son's life. I'd cry about this often. I'd pray for a reconnection with my son and the will of God to allow growth to happen at a natural pace. Here's what happened.

In 2019 I fell in love with the game of golf. There's so much to love about the sport and perhaps I'll one day write a book about the importance of golf in my life. I once read that the all-time great Lawrence Taylor once said that "the game of golf saved my life". When I read that statement, I had never played golf before and so that went over my head but now I completely understand it.

On my phone I have alarms set for prayer reminders. As a Muslim, we are required to pray 5 times per day. One day I'm exiting the golf course, and my alarm goes off. At first, I thought I would just pray in my car before I drove myself home when I heard Allah speak to my soul and say go pray outside your son's home. Being that I haven't seen or spoken to him in 8 years I thought it was an odd request, however I submitted to the will of Allah and obliged. I drove 10 minutes around the corner from the golf course and I prayed outside his home in my truck. I felt incredibly peaceful as I did this and started making that my routine.

Every Sunday I would play that same course and then go pray outside of his home. I did this for months. Not looking for any desired outcome, just enjoying the peace I felt from being in proximity of my estranged son. Eventually, I thought to myself how strange it was to continue this Sunday pattern without ever seeing him. As soon as I had this reflection, I felt the spirit of Allah tell me to break my routine and come back another day. Once again submitting to the will of Allah I obliged. Even though I felt that I was only in the area because I golfed near the house. So why would I go out there if I'm not golfing? That following Tuesday I needed an emergency haircut because I had an upcoming appointment and I wanted to look nice. The barbershop I was attending was 30 minutes past my son's house. As I was returning home from getting my haircut, I felt the spirit of Allah say, "Riley go to the house NOW!" Once again, I thought this was an odd request being that my alarm hadn't sounded off as a reminder that it's time to pray. Prayer time for me wasn't for another 3-4 hours, but I submitted. While I was sitting in my truck wondering why I was there, I felt the spirit ask me "Riley what do you normally do when you're here? I said I pray, and Allah said then PRAY !!!" (I get so emotional thinking of this that I'm crying as I write this out).

Once I finished my prayer, I picked my head up just in time to see the back of the head of a little boy going inside of a house! It happened so fast; I wasn't sure of what I saw. I thought to myself, "did I just see my child for the first time in 8 years?!!" I could not take my eyes off the door I saw that boy walk in. And so, I stared at the door for another 20 minutes and decided to get myself home. My thought was maybe that wasn't him and maybe I didn't see what I thought I saw. When I turned my truck back on, I could feel the spirit of God say turn the truck off and sit still.

My mother always says to me "PEACE be still!" This one statement encouraged restraint.

I asked God for how long and he says just be still! Five minutes later that little boy came back outside with a basketball under his arm. He walked a little way and began to shoot some shots at a nearby court. I started to CRY uncontrollably with one thought swirling in my thoughts: that's my handsome little boy right there who doesn't even know I'm his father because he hasn't been around me since he was 1 year old. The spirit said to me "there's your son right there, now what will you do with what you've been asking for"? The Spirit of God continued as he said, "is seeing him all that you wanted or was there more"? I said with a face full of tears I WANT MORE!! That's when Allah said then do what needs to be done. I approached my son's mother who was outside also sitting in her car as my son was playing on the basketball court. I approached her and could tell she was startled. I requested if we could have some time together to just talk. She agreed, and now long story short I'm able to visit my son occasionally which was way better than not seeing him at all. The moral of this emotional story is I needed to give her space and time to heal. I could not say she should get over everything because I have, that's not my right to do. Much like I explained in the previous chapter. But most importantly, the time spent praying and waiting didn't make sense until it did.

Don't be in a rush to get to a resolution. Instead, let time do its good work on your situation. "Peace, be still."

Tough times and living right
Emotional Intelligence

While everyone faces their own challenges and difficulties in life, individuals who strive to live by their values and maintain their integrity often encounter unique struggles. Making choices aligned with one's principles can sometimes be more challenging than taking shortcuts or compromising on one's principles. However, these challenges can also lead to personal growth, resilience, and a sense of fulfillment in the long run.

I promise you, since taking my Shahada and really striving to live my life with honor and dignity it has been the hardest 5 years of my life. I've cried more in the last 5 years than in all my previous years. The assurance for me is that I know God is REAL and is with me! Some people, who've gone through what I've gone through (without Allah) would make other choices such as abusing drugs, alcohol and possibly even hurting themselves. Praying as often as I do has revealed the fact that just like driven streets my path or journey was designed with potholes and pitfalls. This means I need to build myself up, mentally, spiritually, and physically to take on all that's for me to do while living a righteous existence. If we neglect any of these, we are sure to suffer for it.

Building yourself up mentally is important for several reasons:

Emotional well-being. Strengthening your mental resilience and wellbeing can help you better cope with stress, adversity, and challenges that life throws at you. It allows you to maintain a positive outlook, manage emotions effectively, and bounce back from setbacks.

Self-confidence. Building yourself up mentally can enhance your self-esteem. When you have a positive mindset and believe in your abilities, you are more likely to take on new challenges, pursue your goals, and overcome self-doubt.

Productivity and success. A strong mental foundation enables you to focus, concentrate, and perform at your best. By cultivating good mental habits, such as managing distractions and maintaining motivation, you can enhance your productivity and achieve success in various areas of life.

Relationships. Mental well-being contributes to healthier and more fulfilling relationships. When you are mentally strong, you can communicate effectively, empathize with others, and maintain better emotional balance, leading to stronger connections and deeper understanding.

Adaptability and growth. Building yourself up mentally fosters adaptability and a growth mindset. It helps you embrace change, learn from failures, and see challenges as opportunities for personal development. This mindset allows you to continuously learn, evolve, and reach your full potential.

Overall, investing in your mental well-being empowers you to lead a happier, healthier, and more fulfilling life.

Building yourself up spiritually can be important for several reasons:

>Meaning and Purpose. Spiritual growth helps you explore and discover deeper meaning and purpose in life. It can provide a sense of connection to something greater than yourself and help you find a guiding framework for your values and actions.

>Inner Peace and Well-being. Nurturing your spiritual well-being can lead to a greater sense of inner peace, contentment, and overall well-being. It offers tools and practices, such as meditation, mindfulness, or prayer. Building yourself up spiritually will also promote relaxation, reduce stress, and cultivate a sense of calm.

>Compassion and Empathy. Spiritual development often emphasizes qualities such as compassion, empathy, and kindness towards others. It encourages you to cultivate a deeper understanding of different perspectives, promote harmony, and contribute positively to your community and the world around you.

Resilience and Coping. Resilience and coping can provide you with a source of strength and support during challenging times. It offers a framework for finding solace, hope, and comfort. It helps you navigate adversity, grief, or loss.

Personal Growth and Self-Reflection. Spiritual practices often involve self-reflection, introspection, and self-improvement. They encourage you to examine your thoughts, beliefs, and behaviors, promoting personal growth, self-awareness, and a continuous journey of self-discovery.

Connection and Unity. Building yourself up spiritually can enhance your sense of connection with others, nature, and the universe. It can foster a sense of unity, interconnectedness, and harmony. Helps you develop a broader perspective and a deeper appreciation for the world around you.

Ultimately, spiritual growth is a deeply personal and individual journey, and its importance can vary for different people. It can provide a source of guidance, support, and fulfillment helping you lead a more purposeful and balanced life.

Building yourself up physically is important for several reasons:

Health and Well-being. Physical fitness and strength contribute to overall health and well-being. Regular exercise, proper nutrition, and maintaining a healthy weight can reduce the risk of chronic diseases. There is also the added benefit of improving cardiovascular health, enhancing immune function, and promoting longevity.

Energy and Vitality. Engaging in physical activities and exercise boosts energy levels, improves stamina, and enhances overall vitality. Being physically fit allows you to perform daily tasks with greater ease and enjoy an active lifestyle.

Mental Health. Physical activity has numerous benefits for mental health. It can reduce symptoms of stress, anxiety, depression, improve moods, and promote better sleep. Regular exercise stimulates the release of endorphins which are natural mood-boosting chemicals in the brain.

Strength and Resilience. Physical fitness helps build strength, endurance, and resilience. It improves muscle and bone health, reduces the risk of injuries, and enhances physical performance in various activities or sports.

Self-confidence and Body Image. Taking care of your physical wellbeing can boost self-confidence and improve body image. Feeling strong, fit, and healthy can positively impact self-esteem and promote a positive self-image.

Longevity and Quality of Life. Building physical fitness can contribute to a longer and higher quality of life. Regular exercise and a healthy lifestyle can help prevent age-related decline, maintain mobility and independence, and enhance overall vitality as you age.

Stress Relief. Physical activity serves as an effective outlet for stress relief. Engaging in exercise or sports can help alleviate tension, clear the mind, promote relaxation, and lead to improved mental well-being.

Remember, it's important to consult with healthcare professionals or fitness experts to design a safe and appropriate exercise routine. It should be based on individual abilities, goals, and any specific health considerations.

You're never too old to start a new dream

Emotional Intelligence

Age should never be a barrier to pursuing your dreams or starting something new. It's never too late to embark on a new venture. Learn new skills. Or chase after your passions. With determination, perseverance, and a growth mindset, anyone can work towards building their empire or pursuing a new dream regardless of their age. It's important to believe in yourself and take steps toward your goals no matter where you are in life. The key is to STAY INSPIRED. Going back to a previous chapter, choose and keep the right friends around you.

We've heard so many sayings throughout our lifetime that really are untrue, and they stunt our growth. Such as, "sticks and stones may break my bones, but words can never hurt me." The truth is words from people you love, or respect hurt far more than getting hit with sticks or stones. And sometimes words have the power to make or break you. This is why it's important to use calmness and emotional intelligence when selecting the people who'll have access to you.

There's also the saying "you can't teach an old dog new tricks".

This phrase is an idiom that suggests it is difficult or impossible to teach someone new skills or behaviors especially if they are set in their ways or resistant to change. It is often used to express the belief that older individuals may be less receptive to learning or adapting compared to younger individuals. However, it's important to note that this phrase is not necessarily true and can be misleading. People of any age can continue to learn, grow, and acquire new knowledge and skills if they have the willingness and motivation to do so.

Talk about being an old dog, do you know the inspiring story of Colonel Sanders who created Kentucky Fried Chicken (KFC)? No. Let me share it with you.

Sanders was born in 1890 in Henryville, IN. When he was six years old, his father passed away leaving Sanders to cook and care for his siblings. In seventh grade, he dropped out of school and left home to go work as a farmhand. At 16, he faked his age to enlist in the United States army. After being honorably discharged a year later, he got hired by the railway as a laborer. However, he got fired for fighting with a coworker. While he worked for the railway, he studied law-- until he ruined his legal career by getting into another fight. Sanders was forced to move back in with his mom and get a job selling life insurance. And guess what? He got fired for insubordination. But this guy wouldn't give up. It wasn't until age 40 that he began selling chicken dishes in a service station. As he began to advertise his food (remember he was left to cook for his family since he was 6 years old). His recipe was rejected 1,009 times before anyone accepted it.

Sander's "secret recipe" was coined "Kentucky Fried Chicken", and quickly became a hit.

If you're overwhelmed by rejection or discouraged by setbacks, remember the story of Colonel Harland Sanders. In addition to being fired from multiple jobs, set back by the Great Depression, and World War II; he still created one of the largest fast-food chains in the world as a ripe older man! The moral of the story of this chapter is if you can visualize it GO FOR IT!!!

Peter vs. Judas
Emotional Intelligence

Biblically, Peter's mistake was denying Jesus three times before the rooster crowed, as Jesus had predicted. Peter, despite having a bad day or making mistakes, deserves forgiveness and restoration. Because sometimes we just get it wrong and make the wrong decision. I think the intent of the heart is what really matters. I said earlier how I truly strive to make the right decisions every day, personally or professionally, but I am in no way perfect. I understand that I am flawed and therefore I give those that I'm associated with an abundance of grace. However, Judas's mistake was betraying Jesus by identifying him to the religious authorities for thirty pieces of silver. This act ultimately led to Jesus' arrest and so-called crucifixion. Judas' characterization differs from Peter because Judas had a bad heart. A bad heart is associated with betrayal and may be seen as deserving release or separation. Intentions matter! Judas's intentions are why you release or separate from someone with a bad heart. Judas seems to have made a calculated decision to sacrifice his friend for a few riches.
These stories are examples for us all to learn from. The lesson to be learned from Peter's denial of Jesus in the Bible is the importance of courage, faithfulness, and standing firm in one's convictions, even in the face of adversity or fear. It serves as a reminder of the human capacity for weakness and

the need for repentance and forgiveness. Forgiving someone you love is often the right thing to do, however I wouldn't suggest you give someone the opportunity to continue hurting you. I think the power of forgiveness is undervalued. You can forgive someone and still release them from their place in your life if it becomes necessary.

The story of Judas and Jesus in the Bible teaches several lessons. One important lesson is the destructive power of betrayal and the consequences it can have not only for the one being betrayed but also for the betrayer. It emphasizes the significance of personal responsibility, moral choices, and the importance of genuine remorse and seeking forgiveness. Additionally, it highlights the depth of God's love and willingness to forgive even the gravest of sins. Judas causes us to understand the real value in our relationships. Do they value their relationship with you or are you expendable to them? If you're able to recognize the true value of the relationship, then you'll also recognize when you may become expendable to them. In this case you can use better judgement and remove yourself from an unhealthy situation before you become a pawn for their use.

In the end, just keep in mind Peter had a bad day. Judas had a bad heart. Peter, you restore. Judas you release.

Prepared for the Unpredictable

Emotional Intelligence

There's no predictable blueprint for life's oppositions or opportunities. Our job is to prepare ourselves for the unknown. In other words, life doesn't come with a predetermined plan or set of instructions. It emphasizes the importance of being proactive and ready to face uncertain situations. Instead of relying on a specific roadmap, the focus is on personal preparation, growth, and being adaptable to whatever circumstances arise. It encourages individuals to develop skills, cultivate resilience, and embrace the unknown as part of life's journey.

It also means that there is no predestined path or specific guidelines that apply to everyone's life. Everyone's journey is unique and unfolds in its own way. Unlike a blueprint that provides step-by-step instructions for building or achieving something, life is unpredictable and full of uncertainties. It requires us to make our own choices, face challenges, and navigate through various prospects and problems. We have the freedom and responsibility to shape our own paths and create meaning in our lives, rather than following a predetermined script. It is our job to prepare ourselves for all that may come.

Being proactive and ready to face uncertain situations is important for several reasons:

Adaptability. Uncertainty is a natural part of life and being proactive allows us to adapt quickly to changing circumstances. It helps us remain flexible and open to new possibilities, which is crucial for personal growth and success.

Resilience. Proactively preparing for the unknown builds' resilience. It strengthens our ability to bounce back from setbacks and challenges, enabling us to handle adversity with greater ease and confidence.

Seizing opportunities. Uncertainty can spring forth by unexpected opportunities. By being proactive, we position ourselves to recognize and seize these opportunities when they arise. This proactive mindset allows us to make the most of uncertain situations and potentially achieve our goals.

Empowerment. Being proactive gives us a sense of control and empowerment over our lives. Instead of passively waiting for things to happen, we take charge and actively shape our future. This helps foster a proactive and positive mindset.

Personal growth. Facing uncertainty requires us to step out of our comfort zones and embrace new experiences. By being proactive, we push ourselves to learn, grow, and develop new skills, which leads to personal and professional growth.

Overall, being proactive and ready to face uncertain situations allows us to navigate life's challenges more effectively, find opportunities amidst uncertainty, and cultivate personal resilience and growth.

Thinking Ahead
Emotional Intelligence

The world we live in is changing rapidly every day. It's happening so fast that if you are working to keep up with the times you'll be left behind. Appropriate thinking should be to get ahead of the time.

Thinking ahead of time involves anticipating future possibilities and being proactive in preparing for them. Here are some strategies to help you think ahead:

>Stay informed. Stay updated on current trends, developments, and emerging technologies in your field or area of interest. This allows you to understand potential future changes and adapt accordingly.
>
>Scenario planning. Consider different scenarios and their potential impact on your goals or plans. Explore best-case, worst-case, and various in-between scenarios. This helps you identify potential challenges and opportunities and develop strategies to address them.
>
>Develop foresight skills. Cultivate your ability to think critically, analyze trends, and make informed predictions about the future. Study historical

patterns, engage in future-focused discussions, and seek out diverse perspectives to enhance your foresight abilities.

Set goals and create a roadmap. Define your long-term goals and create a roadmap that outlines the steps needed to achieve them. By setting clear objectives and breaking them down into actionable tasks, you can better plan and work towards your desired outcomes.

Embrace innovation and change. Be open to new ideas, technologies, and ways of doing things. Embracing innovation and change allows you to stay ahead of the curve and adapt to evolving circumstances.

Continuously learn and develop skills. Invest in lifelong learning to stay relevant and acquire new skills. Develop a growth mindset that embraces personal and professional development, enabling you to adapt to future challenges and seize opportunities.

Thinking ahead of time requires a combination of foresight, adaptability, and proactive planning. By incorporating these strategies into your mindset and approach, you can better prepare for the future and navigate uncertainties with confidence.

Obscurity is Acceptable

Emotional Intelligence

It's perfectly acceptable to not constantly seek attention or be in the spotlight. Attention can be like a drug to an addict. The more you get it the more you seek it and without it you feel the loss and need for more of it. I've been getting attention since I was a young boy (as young as 7years old) and that attention escalated when I turned 14 years old. From the age of 14 to 22 I was being written about (newspapers and magazines) constantly as I was developing into a pretty good basketball player. With that attention came other people's expectations of me as I tried to live up to all things. I've learned to step away and learn myself. I go to places where nobody knows me. I enjoy the solitude of being alone and meditating. I'm so surprised at how deep I can dive into my own mental when I'm focusing on personal growth and development. I've learned that being "on the scene" can stunt my own growth and I'm curious to see what kind of man I can become.

Here are a few reasons why this perspective can be valuable:

> Personal Space. Everyone needs personal space and time for themselves. It's important to have moments

of privacy, solitude, and reflection without feeling the pressure to always be visible or available to others.

Introversion. Introverted individuals often find solace and recharge their energy by spending time alone. It's perfectly fine to prioritize one's own needs for introspection and self-care rather than constantly seeking external validation or attention.

Focus on Personal Growth. Taking a step back from constant visibility can provide an opportunity to focus on personal growth, set goals, and work towards self-improvement without distractions or the need for constant validation from others.

Authenticity. Being constantly visible or seeking attention can sometimes lead to a sense of pressure to maintain a certain image or conform to others' expectations. Embracing the idea that it's okay not to be seen all the time allows individuals to be authentic and true to themselves, without the need to constantly perform for others.

Boundaries. Setting boundaries and knowing when to step back from the limelight can help maintain a healthy work-life balance and prevent burnout. It allows individuals to prioritize their well-being and ensure that their personal needs are met.

It's okay to take breaks, have moments of privacy, and focus on personal growth without feeling the need to be seen or seek constant attention.

Strong Crews
Emotional Intelligence

A circle without constructive criticism is where enabling gets mistaken for support and "yes men" get mistaken as friends. This statement highlights the importance of Constructive Criticism within a strong crew or team.
How do you criticize people you love? Why is this important? Let's deal with the first question.

Constructive Criticism involves:

> Identifying weaknesses. Strong crews are composed of individuals who can recognize and acknowledge each other's weaknesses. By doing so, they can work together to address those weaknesses and improve their overall performance.
>
> Strengthening strengths. By pointing out weaknesses, crew members can help each other grow and develop. This process allows individuals to focus on honing their strengths and becoming even better in their respective areas of expertise.
>
> Differentiating support from enabling. Constructive criticism helps prevent enabling behavior, where individuals may unknowingly hinder personal growth by providing only positive feedback. By offering

honest and constructive criticism, crew members prioritize genuine support and growth over temporary comfort.

Avoiding "yes men". In a circle without constructive criticism, people may surround themselves with individuals who always agree with them, often referred to as "yes men." While it may seem supportive, this can hinder personal and collective growth. Constructive criticism challenges ideas and encourages diverse perspectives, leading to better decision making and innovation.

By fostering an environment where constructive criticism is valued and encouraged, strong crews can collectively improve their skills, support genuine growth, and avoid the pitfalls of enabling behavior or surrounding themselves with "yes men." It promotes a culture of continuous improvement and collaboration. Strong Crews can point out each other's weaknesses to harden their strengths.

Now onto why constructive criticism is so important. Constructive criticism is important for several reasons:

> Personal growth and improvement. Constructive criticism provides valuable feedback that helps individuals identify areas for improvement. It offers specific suggestions or insights that can be used to

enhance skills, knowledge, and performance in various aspects of life.

Enhanced self-awareness. Constructive criticism allows individuals to gain a deeper understanding of their strengths, weaknesses, and blind spots. It helps them develop self-awareness, which is essential for personal and professional development.

Better decision-making. Constructive criticism challenges assumptions and offers alternative perspectives. It helps individuals see different angles of a situation, leading to more informed and well-rounded decision making.

Building strong relationships. Constructive criticism, when delivered with empathy and respect, strengthens relationships. It promotes open communication and trust, as it shows that individuals genuinely care about each other's growth and success.

Continuous learning. Constructive criticism encourages a growth mindset and a desire for continuous learning. It fosters an environment where individuals are open to feedback, willing to learn from their mistakes, and constantly seeking ways to improve.

Innovation and creativity. Constructive criticism supports individuals to think outside the box, challenge existing ideas, and explore new possibilities. It fosters an environment that promotes innovation, creativity, and the generation of fresh ideas.

Professional development. In professional settings, constructive criticism plays a vital role in career advancement. It helps individuals identify areas to focus on for skill development, which can lead to increased opportunities for growth and advancement.

Overall, constructive criticism serves as a catalyst for personal growth, self-improvement, better decision-making, and fostering strong relationships. By embracing and incorporating constructive feedback, individuals can continuously learn, adapt, and evolve in both personal and professional aspects of life.

Betrayal is a part of the Plan

Emotional Intelligence

Masha'Allah, Ma shaa **Allah** is an Arabic phrase that means "God has willed" or "as God willing".
In Islam, we are taught to acknowledge the blessing of Allah in everything in our lives (good or bad)
Reflectively, this statement is a philosophical perspective that suggests even negative actions or betrayals can serve a larger purpose or plan. It draws a parallel to the biblical story of Jesus and Judas, implying that Judas' betrayal was necessary for Jesus' crucifixion and ultimate redemption.
It's a thought-provoking concept that reminds us and highlights the interconnectedness of events and the potential for unexpected outcomes.

The theory of right and wrong is Timeless

Emotional Intelligence

Morality or right and wrong are not bound by a specific timetable or time limit. They are universal principles that guide ethical judgment and behavior regardless of time or circumstance. These principles are considered universal because they apply across different cultures, societies, and time periods.

For example, actions like honesty, fairness, and respect for others are generally regarded as morally right, while actions like lying, cheating, and harming others are considered morally wrong. These principles guide ethical judgment and behavior, serving as a honorable compass for individuals and societies. Regardless of the era or culture, the constancy of what is right and wrong helps to establish a foundation for moral decision-making and provide a framework for individuals to navigate their actions and choices.

Daily opportunities abound to make right or wrong decisions. However, the "grey" area of these choices comes when you are forced to weigh the decisions against your needs. For example, if you're facing an eviction on Friday and you decide to do something illegal to make the rent; you were forced into a situation that caused you to look past your own morals. Too often we find ourselves in situations that may jeopardize our ethics to satisfy a need or want. I believe in Karma. There's a saying that goes "if you tell a lie, you must

remember the lie you told and stand on it" it becomes difficult to memorize the lie as you tell it to more people. I've found life to be easier when you've made a routine of doing what's right. Starting your day with prayer, exercise, and feeding your brain positive and fruitful substance. Taking time to meditate, along with communicating with your family and letting them know how much they mean to you. Or simply going to work and executing your duties to the best of your ability makes it almost impossible for you to have a bad day.
Start your positive routine today!

Every choice comes with an invoice

Emotional Intelligence

Choices remind us to consider the potential costs and benefits before making decisions. Considering the likely expense and advantages or disadvantages before committing an act is a wise approach to life. By carefully weighing the probable outcomes, we can make more informed choices that align with our goals and values. It allows us to anticipate and evaluate the potential risks and rewards associated with each decision. This helps us make choices that are more likely to lead to positive outcomes.

I've made a career out of being patient and allowing situations to calmly play themselves out. Sometimes this is a great strategy, and I can say I've benefited from my patience more times than not. However, there are also times that I've been too patient and possibly lost opportunities.

Understanding there are consequences that come with our actions, I'm reminded of stories in my life where I was willing to deal with the consequences of my actions regarding some major decisions. My high school basketball Coach (Hank Galotta) once said to me "Riley, you never made any excuses. Whatever choices you ever made, I always saw you stand up with your chin high and with grace, and deal with the consequences I believe this strength came from my mother! I never heard my mother say she could not deal with what was going on in her life. The one thing I knew was she was willing to swing back at challenges no matter how hard the fight may have seemed. This trait is definitively instilled in me! For example, attending Mount Saint Mary College versus a High Major. Coming out of high school, I was a 6'2.5-point guard, 4-year varsity basketball starter with division 1 offers ringing in from division 1 schools up and down the east coast. I was recruited by universities in the ACC, Big East, Big 10, A-10, and SEC. Yet, I'd end up playing college basketball at Mount Saint Mary's University and we'd compete in the NEC (North Eastern Conference). Additionally, I believed I was an NBA prospect with my size, skill set, and basketball IQ. In those days to seal this deal I should've attended one of the high major division 1 schools and played along with some other great players. But there was so much going on in my life at this time that I lost focus of that NBA goal. Well, that's not exactly true. I also had what you would call athletic arrogance about myself. I believed I was good enough to play in the NBA and it didn't matter what college I attended. This choice came with an invoice! The demand of that decision positioned me with something no other school in America had. Coach Don Anderson. I discovered I needed his patience, his guidance, and his love. When I arrived at his program, I was a broken and confused boy at 18 years old. In the end, being a great man and future father would be more valuable and important to me than playing in the NBA. I needed Don Anderson to become the man that I am today.

My choice to attend MSM for the human development was my decision and the invoice would be attending a school that did not prepare me to play at the highest level. For a while, I thought both things were possible, but I needed a different, more selfish approach to pull that off and that's just not me. To be sure, I wouldn't go back and change the choice I made. Reader, stand 10 toes down on whatever choice you make. Be prepared to carry out the demands of those decisions no matter what they are.

These things you must master: Understanding, Forgiveness, and Love

Understanding, forgiveness, and Love are indeed important qualities to cultivate and master in life. *Understanding* allows us to empathize and see things from different perspectives, fostering harmony and compassion. *Forgiveness* frees us from the burden of holding grudges, promoting healing and personal growth. And *Love*, the most powerful force of all, can transform lives and create deep connections. By mastering these qualities, we can enhance our relationships, promote peace within ourselves, and make a positive impact on the world around us.

Let's delve deeper.

Understanding is crucial because it forms the foundation for empathy, compassion, and effective communication. When we seek to understand others, we open ourselves to different viewpoints, experiences, and emotions. It allows us to see beyond our own perspectives and biases, fostering tolerance and acceptance. Because understanding promotes empathy, we are enabled to relate to others' joys, sorrows, and challenges. It helps build connections and deepens relationships. We can truly see and appreciate others for who they are. With understanding, we can bridge divides, resolve conflicts, and promote harmony in various aspects of life. From personal relationships, workplace dynamics, or global interactions. Moreover, understanding is essential for effective communication. It helps us listen attentively, ask meaningful questions, and respond thoughtfully. When we understand others, we can convey our thoughts and feelings more effectively fostering mutual perception and cooperation. Overall, understanding cultivates compassion, empathy, and open-mindedness, leading to more harmonious relationships, personal growth, and a more inclusive and understanding society.

Forgiveness is important for our emotional well-being, personal growth, and the health of our relationships. Here are a few reasons why forgiveness holds such significance:

> Emotional Healing. Forgiveness allows us to let go of negative emotions such as anger, resentment, and bitterness. By releasing these emotions, we free ourselves from the burden of carrying grudges, which can be emotionally draining and detrimental to our mental health.

Personal Growth. Forgiveness plays a vital role in our personal growth and development. It requires us to reflect on our own flaws and shortcomings, fostering humility and self-awareness. Through forgiveness, we can learn from our mistakes and become better versions of ourselves.

Relationship Repair. Forgiveness is often a crucial step in repairing damaged relationships. It helps to rebuild trust, foster empathy, and promote reconciliation. By forgiving others, we create space for healing, understanding, and the possibility of restoring meaningful connections.

Inner Peace. Holding onto anger and resentment can consume our thoughts and affect our overall well-being. Forgiveness brings inner peace by freeing us from negativity and allowing us to focus on the positive aspects of life. It promotes a sense of serenity and contentment.

Emotional Resilience. Forgiveness strengthens our emotional resilience. It enables us to navigate conflicts and setbacks with grace and compassion. By choosing forgiveness, we cultivate emotional strength and the ability to move forward, even in challenging circumstances.

It's important to note that forgiveness does not mean condoning or forgetting hurtful actions. It's a personal choice to let go of negative emotions and find healing, both for us and our relationships.

Love is the last and essential aspect to master because it is a powerful force that has the potential to bring about positive change and transformation in ourselves and others.

Here are a few reasons why Love holds such importance:

>Connection and Empathy. Love allows us to form deep connections with others, fostering empathy and compassion. It enables us to understand and resonate with the joys, sorrows, and experiences of others, promoting a sense of unity and shared humanity.

>Healing and Growth. Love has the power to heal emotional wounds and promote personal growth. It creates an environment of acceptance, support, and understanding, enabling individuals to feel safe to express themselves authentically. Love nurtures self-esteem, resilience, and the courage to embrace vulnerability.

>Positive Relationships. Love is the foundation of healthy and fulfilling relationships. It cultivates trust, respect, and appreciation for one another. When love is present in relationships, it encourages open

communication, forgiveness, and the willingness to work through challenges together.

Social Harmony. Love extends beyond individual relationships and plays a vital role in creating a harmonious society. It encourages kindness, empathy, and cooperation among people. Love promotes inclusivity, acceptance, and the recognition of the inherent worth of all individuals.

Personal Well-being. Love contributes to our overall well-being and happiness. When we experience love, whether it's self-love or love from others, it boosts our mood, reduces stress, and enhances our mental and emotional health. Love provides a sense of purpose, fulfillment, and joy in life.

By mastering understanding, forgiveness, and love, we become agents of positive change. In other words, possessing these three allows compassion, kindness, and empathy to be spread abroad. Simultaneously we create meaningful connections, experience personal growth, and contribute to a more loving and harmonious society.

Final Thoughts

"The man who views the world at 50 the same as he did at 20 has wasted 30 years of his life,"

This quote, from the 1975 issue of Playboy Magazine, is often attributed to Muhammad Ali, the renowned boxer and cultural icon. It conveys the idea that personal growth and evolving perspectives are important aspects of life. By suggesting that an individual who maintains the same worldview over a span of 30 years has wasted their time, Ali emphasizes the value of learning, maturing, and broadening one's understanding of the world.

I once read this quote as a boy, and it has always stayed with me. I learned that it's important that we are evolving constantly because if not, we've wasted the gift of Allah and that's the ability to evolve into much more. We are boundless beings if we're willing to stretch our mental as well as our physical. This book is about my evolution in the last 30 years and the lessons I've documented mentally and learned from. I hope some of these lessons bless and fill your spirit like meatloaf.

WHOUWITT

About the Author

Riley, is a true Knicks fan at heart.
He enjoys a good laugh with his family and friends,
and believes Jermaine is the real talent of the Jackson family.

Made in the USA
Middletown, DE
14 March 2024